Contents

Teachers' notes	1	From steam to water	18
Notes on individual activities	2	Where does water come from?	19
What is water like?	5	Make a rain gauge	20
What do we use water for?	6	Keeping ice cubes cold	21
What shape is water?	7	An ice cube melting	22
Running water	8	Dissolving things in water	23
Water level	9	Dilute a drink	24
Make a siphon	10	Floating and sinking	25
Water surface	11	Pushing water	26
A drop of water	12	Jets of water	27
Drops of water on surfaces	13	Do seeds need water to grow?	28
Washing hands	14	Do plants take up water?	29
Puddle puzzle	15	What did I drink today?	30
Water disappears into the air	16	Make a water filter	31
The best weather for drying	17	Water in our homes	32

Teachers' notes

Aims of this book

The aims of this book are:
- To raise awareness of the various uses of water.
- To examine some of the properties of water, for example: water takes the shape of its container; water flows until it reaches a common level; some objects float in water, others sink; some substances dissolve in water; water evaporates; heating and cooling causes water to change.
- To show that the force of water can move things.
- To show that the surface of water has a tension.
- To demonstrate that water pressure increases with depth.
- To demonstrate that plants need water.
- To raise awareness of the different forms of water in a variety of weather conditions.
- To show where water in the tap comes from.
- To introduce the idea of the water cycle.
- To demonstrate that water can be cleaned.

Safety precautions

The activities described on the worksheets mainly use everyday items of equipment and materials which are perfectly safe if used sensibly. Where extra care is necessary on safety grounds, this is mentioned both on the worksheets and also in the appropriate section of the teachers' notes.

Scientific background

This information is intended to help you to understand the scientific concepts covered in this book. It goes beyond the level of understanding expected of most children, but it will give you the confidence to ask and answer questions and to guide the children in their investigations. Further information is contained in the worksheet notes.

Water

Water is a compound made of the gases hydrogen and oxygen. It is the most common substance on Earth, covering about 70 per cent of its surface. The heat from the Sun causes water to evaporate into the air, both from wet surfaces such as oceans, seas, rivers and puddles, and from trees and other plants. The water rises as vapour. As it cools, it condenses, forming tiny droplets of water which are seen as clouds. The clouds are carried along in currents of air. Rain falls when the droplets cool and join together to form larger drops. If the air is very cold, the rain may fall as snow, hail or sleet. When the water falls, it soaks through the soil and rock, forming springs, or drains into streams. The springs and streams merge, forming rivers which flow back to the sea and the oceans. This process is called the water cycle.

Water boils at 100°C, forming water vapour. We see steam when droplets form as the water vapour condenses. Water freezes at 0°C, forming ice. Ice floats as it is less dense than water.

Water is essential for all living things. Living things are made up of large amounts of water. The human body is roughly 70 per cent water.

The surface tension of water draws water inwards so that when drops are formed, they are rounded. Water flows from a tap in a rounded stream. The surface tension causes some objects that would otherwise sink to stay on the surface.

Notes on individual activities

Page 5: What is water like?

Key idea: clean tap water is colourless, does not smell and has no taste. It feels 'wet'.
Extension activity: let the children collect rain-water or river-water to compare different sources of water. **Safety precautions:** do not let them taste rain- or river-water and remind them to wash their hands after touching the water.

Page 6: What do we use water for?

Key idea: water is necessary for us to live. We use water in many ways.
Developing the investigation: discuss with the children the ways in which we use water during the day. Let them discuss the pictures and encourage them to add their own ideas. The children can go on to contribute to a class frieze showing the ways water is used in school.

Page 7: What shape is water?

Key idea: water is liquid. It takes the shape of whatever contains it.
Developing the investigation: ask the children to make a collection of different containers, e.g. a twisty drinking straw or a plastic container with a hollow handle, and fill them with water.

Page 8: Running water

Key idea: water flows to find its own level.
Likely outcome: water running down a slope will form a narrow stream. Water on a flat surface will form a puddle.
Developing the investigation: ask the children to observe what happens when there is something in the path of water. Show pictures of rivers, lakes and the sea. Discuss how the water is moving. Have the children experienced flooding? Why does a river flood?

Page 9: Water level

Key idea: water finds its own level.
Likely outcome: water in the tubing will always be at the same level on each side because water will always be at the lowest level possible.
Extension activity: explain how water runs out of a tap. At home, water is stored in a tank which is above the level of the taps.

Page 10: Make a siphon

Key idea: air pressure on the surface of water forces the water to move up the pipe.
Likely outcome: water will flow through the tube until the water levels are the same in both bowls. (Make sure there are no air bubbles left in the tube when it is pushed under water.)
Extension activities: let the children find out what happens if the end of the tube in the lower bowl is raised. How high can the tube be raised between the bowls – does the water continue to flow through? Discuss how the air is pushing down on the surface of water in the higher bowl.

Page 11: Water surface

Key idea: surface tension provides enough force to prevent the water from overflowing.
Likely outcome: children will be able to see the curved edge of the water as they drop the counters in.
Developing the investigation: discuss how the surface of water can support some pond animals such as pond skaters.

Page 12: A drop of water

Key idea: water surface tension holds the drop of water in a curved shape. A drop of water can act as a magnifier.
Likely outcome: children will see the curved edge of a drop of water and find out how many drops they can add to the original drop before the surface tension breaks and the water flows.

Page 13: Drops of water on surfaces

Key idea: some materials absorb water, others do not.
Likely outcome: foil, plastic and waxed paper will not absorb water. Other materials will.
Developing the investigation: discuss the word 'absorb' and 'absorption'. Talk about things used to absorb water, e.g. sponges and paper towels.

Page 14: Washing hands

Key idea: we use water for washing. Warm water and soap make washing more effective.
Extension activity: let the children make the same investigation using different substances to make 'dirty' hands such as paint or newsprint.

Page 15: Puddle puzzle

Key idea: water evaporates.
Extension activity: give the children two containers such as a bowl and a plastic bottle. Let them monitor evaporation over time.

Page 16: Water disappears into the air

Key idea: water evaporates into the air.
Likely outcome: the beaker of water with the plastic cover will weigh more because the plastic film will prevent the water vapour from escaping into the air.
Developing the investigation: discuss with the

children how water seems to disappear as things dry. Explain the word 'evaporate'. Water is in the air as a vapour which we cannot see.

Page 17: The best weather for drying

Key idea: the weather affects how quickly water evaporates.
Likely outcome: more water will have evaporated in sunny, windy weather.
Developing the investigation: ask the children what has happened to the water. Do they think large amounts of water evaporate from the sea?

Page 18: From steam to water

Key idea: steam is tiny droplets of water in the air. When steam touches something cold it condenses and becomes water.
Likely outcome: when steam touches the ladle it will mist up the surface and then form drops of water.
Extension activity: discuss the different types of machines which use steam power.
Safety precautions: when working with hot water, children should be supervised at all times.

Page 19: Where does water come from?

Key idea: the water in our taps is part of the water cycle.
Developing the investigation: discuss how water evaporates, especially when the sun is shining on the surface of the water, forming water vapour which we cannot see. The air cools, droplets form and join, forming larger drops which fall as rain. Rain eventually flows into rivers.

Page 20: Make a rain gauge

Key idea: water falls as rain. Rainfall can be measured over a period of time.
Developing the investigation: discuss weather and weather forecasting with the children. Let them look out for rain clouds.

Page 21: Keeping ice cubes cold

Key idea: insulators such as woollen fabric, newspaper or polystyrene can help to keep substances cool.
Likely outcome: the unwrapped ice cube will melt first.
Developing the investigation: discuss how we keep things cool. When we go on a picnic we use a cool box. What is the cool box lined with? (Frequently it is expanded polystyrene.)

Page 22: An ice cube melting

Key idea: ice is frozen water. When ice is warmed it becomes water again. Some substances such as salt speed the melting.
Likely outcome: the ice will slowly melt. Remind the children to look at the melting ice at intervals.
Developing the investigation: talk about freezing water with the children. Where do we freeze water? Let them feel an ice cube and look at it with a hand lens.

Page 23: Dissolving things in water

Key idea: some substances dissolve in water. Others sink to the bottom.
Developing the investigation: discuss what we mean by the word 'dissolve'. Put a teaspoon of instant coffee into hot water. Let the children see what happens. Decide with the children whether each beaker will be stirred.

Page 24: Dilute a drink

Key idea: water can be added to dilute a solution.
Likely outcome: the taste and colour will change as more water is added.
Developing the investigation: discuss the words 'dilute' and 'concentrated' with the children. Which drinks do they have at home which need to be diluted?

Page 25: Floating and sinking

Key idea: some objects float in water, others sink.
Developing the investigation: test out further ideas, such as do all wooden things float or do all glass things sink? Do some things which are empty float and some things which are full of water sink? Can the children make any of the floaters sink or sinkers float?

Page 26: Pushing water

Key idea: water exerts an upward pressure, or upthrust, on floating objects, and this can be felt. Floating objects displace water.
Likely outcome: the harder the floating ball is pressed down into the water, the harder the water seems to be pushing upwards. Each ball displaces its own weight of water, and this causes the water level in the bucket to rise.
Extension activities: discuss the use of lifebuoys, inflatable arm-bands and life-jackets.

Page 27: Jugs of water

Key idea: water presses down. The pressure increases with the depth of water.
Likely outcome: the water jet from the bottle with the hole near the base has more force because of the greater pressure from the weight of water.
Extension activity: let the children make two or three holes in a line down another squeezy bottle. Ask them how the water will jet out of the holes. Let them find out.

Page 28: Do seeds need water to grow?

Key idea: seeds need water to grow.
Likely outcome: the seeds in the beaker containing water will germinate. The others will not.

Developing the investigation: discuss what seeds and plants need to grow. Let the children continue to grow the seeds.

Page 29: Do plants take up water?

Key idea: plants take up water through their stems.
Likely outcome: the coloured water will be visible in the celery stem. The flower may change to the colour of the water.
Developing the investigation: discuss what plants need to live. Ask how the children think the water gets into the plant.

Page 30: What did I drink today?

Key idea: we need water to stay healthy. Things we drink and many things we eat contain large amounts of water.
Developing the investigation: ask the children to compare the records they make. Ask them how they could find out how much they drink in a day.

Page 31: Making a water filter

Key idea: filtering water helps to purify it.
Likely outcome: the water will be visibly cleaner after it has passed through the filter.
Developing the investigation: discuss with the children how water is pumped from rivers and reservoirs to the waterworks. At the waterworks the water is cleaned in a series of processes including a filter bed. Send for information from your local water board.

Page 32: Water in our homes

Key idea: clean water is piped to our homes from the water mains and used water is piped away through waste pipes to the sewer.
Developing the investigation: take the children to see the water mains in the school and discover where the waste pipes go to the main sewer. Take the children to a sewage plant if possible.
Extension activity: ask the children how they could save water.

National Curriculum: Science

In addition to the PoS for AT1, the following PoS of the National Curriculum for science are relevant to this book:

Life processes and living things
Pupils should be taught:
▲ that humans need food and water to stay alive;
▲ that plants need light and water to grow.

Materials and their properties
Pupils should be taught:
▲ to use their senses to explore and recognise the similarities and differences between materials;
▲ to sort materials into groups on the basis of simple properties;
▲ that many materials have a variety of uses;
▲ that materials are chosen for specific uses on the basis of their properties;
▲ that objects made from some materials can be changed in shape by processes;
▲ to describe the way some everyday materials change when they are heated or cooled.

Physical processes
Pupils should be taught:
▲ to describe the movement of familiar things;
▲ that both pushes and pulls are example of forces;
▲ that forces can make things speed up, slow down or change direction;
▲ that forces can change the shapes of objects.

Scottish 5 – 14 Curriculum: Environmental studies

Attainment outcomes	Strands
Science in the environment	Processes of life; energy; forces; materials; planet Earth; weather and climate
Living with technology	Technology and needs; technology, design and control
Health and safe living	Looking after myself; my environment
Investigating	Planning; finding out; recording; interpreting; reporting
Positive attitudes to the environment	Conservation and avoiding waste

▲ Name _____

What is water like?

You will need: a beaker of clean water from the tap.

▲ How many things can you find out about water, using your senses?

What does water look like?

Can you see through the clean water?

Does water smell?

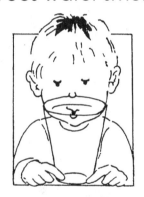

Has it a taste?

What does water feel like?

Does still water make a sound?

▲ Dip your fingers in the water and let the drops fall back into the water. Do the drops make a sound?

▲ Is there anything else you can find out about water using your senses?

▲ ESSENTIALS FOR SCIENCE: Water

▲ Name _____

What do we use water for?

▲ Colour the parts of the picture that show how we use water.

▲ Think of other ways in which water is used. Add your own pictures or make a list on the back of this sheet.

▲ ESSENTIALS FOR SCIENCE: Water

▲ Name _____

What shape is water?

You will need: a jug of water; other containers of different shapes.

▲ What shape is the water in the jug?

▲ Pour the water into another container. What shape is the water now?

▲ What shape will the water be when you pour it into other containers?

▲ What does this tell you about the shape of water?

▲ Draw the containers and water below.

▲ Name _____

Running water

You will need: jugs of water; a plastic tray or a piece of guttering.

▲ Make a slope with the plastic tray or the piece of guttering.

▲ If you pour water gently, which way do you think it will run? Pour the water slowly and watch.

▲ Will water move in the same way on a flat surface?

▲ Lay the tray or guttering flat and try it. Did the water run where you expected?

▲ In the space below, draw the pathway of the water on the sloping and the flat surface.

▲ What have you found out about water?

On the slope	On flat ground

▲ ESSENTIALS FOR SCIENCE: Water

▲ Name _____

Water level

You will need: a length of clear tubing; a funnel; a jug of water.

Work with a partner.

▲ Push the end of the funnel into one end of the tubing.

▲ Ask a friend to pour water into the funnel while you hold the tubing in a U shape.

▲ What do you notice about the water levels on either side of the tubing?

▲ Raise one side of the tubing and then lower it. What do you notice about the water level?

▲ In the tube below, draw in the water level.

▲ Add your own drawings of ways you changed the shape of the tubing. Put the water levels in your drawings.

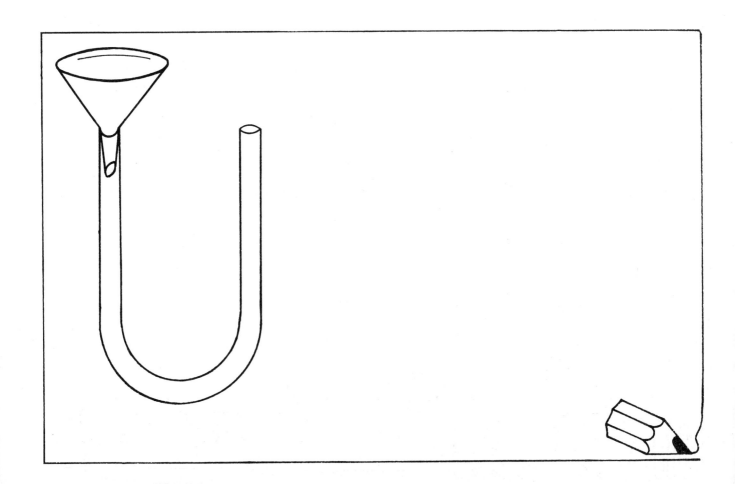

▲ ESSENTIALS FOR SCIENCE: Water

Make a siphon

You will need: two bowls; a length of tubing; water.

Work with a friend.

▲ Fill one bowl with water and place it higher than the second bowl.

▲ Push one end of the tubing under the water in the higher bowl.

▲ Fill the tubing with water but keep your thumb over the end so that it doesn't pour out.

▲ Place the end with your thumb over it in the lower bowl. Release your thumb.

▲ You have made a siphon. What is pushing the water along the tube?

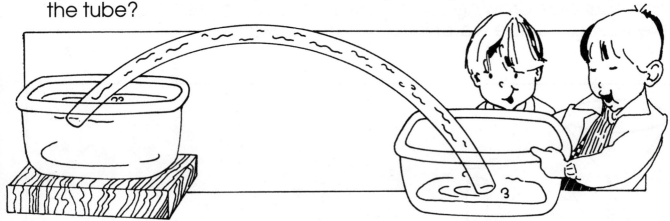

▲ Draw the levels of water in the picture below to show what happens.

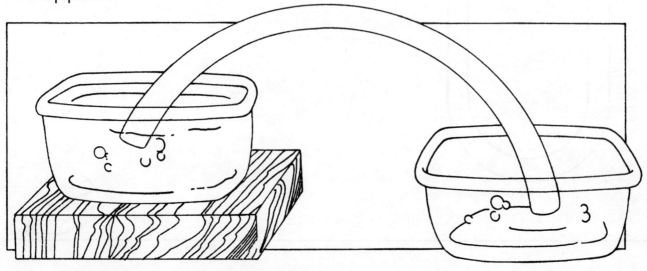

▲ Name _____

Water surface

You will need: a clear beaker; water; plastic counters.

▲ Fill the beaker to the brim with water.

▲ Look at the surface of the water.

▲ Slip counters into the water.

▲ Watch what happens to the surface of the water.

▲ Add more counters.

▲ Watch how the surface of the water curves up above the rim of the beaker.

▲ How many counters can you put in the glass before it overflows?

▲ The surface of water can hold up things which would otherwise sink.

▲ Lay a small plastic counter on the surface of the water. Can you make it stay there?

▲ ESSENTIALS FOR SCIENCE: Water

▲ Name _____

A drop of water

You will need: a plastic dropper; a beaker of water; a clear plastic lid (Petri dish); a hand lens.

▲ Learn how to use the dropper. Then put one drop of water on the plastic lid.

▲ Use the hand lens to look closely at the water.

▲ Add two more drops and look closely again. Can you see the curved edge of the blob of water?

▲ How many drops do you need to add to the blob before it overflows and changes shape?

▲ Draw and write about what you saw.

1 drop	3 drops	More drops

▲ Lift up the lid and hold it over some writing. What do you notice about the writing when you look through the water?

▲ What else can you find out about a drop of water?

▲ ESSENTIALS FOR SCIENCE: Water

▲ Name _____

Drops of water on surfaces

You will need: a plastic dropper; a hand lens; a jug of water; glue; small pieces of each of the following: foil, plastic bag, waxed paper, kitchen roll, newspaper, art paper.

Work with a friend.

▲ Drop one or two drops of water on each material. What happens?

▲ Use a hand lens to see clearly. Which materials soak up water?

▲ Divide the materials into two sets and list them on the chart below.

These absorbed water	These did not absorb water

▲ Find some more materials to test. Add them to the chart.

▲ ESSENTIALS FOR SCIENCE: Water

▲ Name _____

Washing hands

You will need: cold water; hand-hot water; soap; paper towels; a clock timer.

Work with two friends.

▲ One person will be the time-keeper. The other two should make their hands muddy.

▲ Now one person should get ready to wash their hands in cold water and the other in hot water.

▲ Start the timer. Wash the hands for half a minute. Whose hands are the cleanest?

▲ Now try again using soap as well for half a minute.

▲ What have you found out? Draw and write about it in the spaces below.

Cold water	**Hot water**
Cold water and soap 	**Hot water and soap** 

▲ What would happen if you washed your hands in coloured water?

▲ ESSENTIALS FOR SCIENCE: Water

Puddle puzzle

You will need: a jug of water; a plastic sheet; chalk; a felt-tipped pen.

Work with a friend. Choose a sunny day.

▲ After it has rained, make a chalk mark round the edge of a puddle.

▲ Draw round it again later.
  • Has the size of the puddle changed?
  • Where has the water gone?
  • Could the water have gone into the ground?

▲ Now put the plastic sheet on the ground and pour on water to make a puddle. Draw round this puddle with a felt-tipped pen.

▲ Draw round it again later.
  • Has the size of the puddle changed?
  • Where has the water gone?

▲ Draw and write about it below.

▲ Draw your puddle with the chalk marks to show how the puddle has changed.

ESSENTIALS FOR SCIENCE: Water

▲ Name _____

Water disappears into the air

You will need: balance scales; two clear plastic beakers; a dropper; plastic film.

Work with a friend.

▲ Pour exactly the same amount of water into the two beakers.

▲ Put them on the balance scales and add drops of water to the lighter beaker until they balance.

▲ Now cover one of the beakers with plastic film.

▲ Leave the beakers on the balance scales for a day. Do the beakers still weigh the same?

▲ What has happened to the water in the lighter beaker?

▲ Draw the balance scales and beakers on the first day and on the second day.

day 1	day 2

▲ Find out what happens if you leave the beakers for several days.

▲ Name _____

The best weather for drying

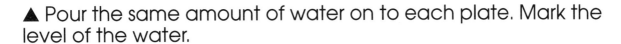

You will need: two plates; a measuring jug.

Work with a friend.

▲ Put one plate in a sunny spot outside and the other in a shady spot outside.

▲ Pour the same amount of water on to each plate. Mark the level of the water.

▲ Leave for a few hours and then check what has happened.

▲ What did you find out? Write and draw about it below.

In the sun   **In the shade**

▲ Try the same experiment on a windy day. Put one plate in an exposed position and the other in a sheltered position. Record what happened below.

In the wind   **Out of the wind**

▲ Name _____

From steam to water

You will need: a kettle of boiling water; a ladle or a tablespoon.

Ask an adult to carry out this experiment.

▲ What is steam? Watch the steam rising from a boiling kettle.
Steam is hot. Do not try to touch it.

▲ Ask an adult to hold a ladle or a spoon against the steam. What happens?

▲ Hold the ladle away from the kettle. When it is cold touch it.
 • What can you see and feel?
 • What has happened to the steam?

▲ In the space below, draw and label what happened to the steam when it touched the ladle.

The steam changed into water on the ladle.

▲ Could you turn the water into steam again?

▲ ESSENTIALS FOR SCIENCE: Water

▲ Name _____

Where does water come from?

Work with your friends.

▲ Look at the picture below. Talk about what is in the picture.

▲ Colour in the sun and the water.

▲ Put arrows to show which way the water is moving. Which way will the arrows point when the sun is shining on the water?

▲ Follow the water cycle to find out how the water gets to your taps.

▲ Do you think the same water is used over and over again?

▲ ESSENTIALS FOR SCIENCE: Water

▲ Name _____

Make a rain gauge

You will need: a clear plastic bottle; scissors.

Ask an adult to help.

▲ Cut off the top section of the plastic bottle.

▲ Turn it upside down and put it in the base.

▲ Stand the rain gauge in open ground.

▲ Each day check how much water has collected in the rain gauge.

▲ Keep a record for a week.

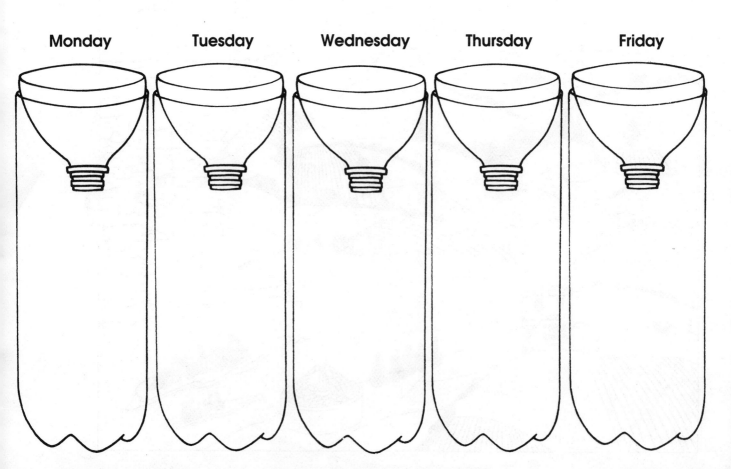

▲ How much rain fell in the week?

▲ Compare this rainfall with the weekly rainfall during another season of the year.

▲ ESSENTIALS FOR SCIENCE: Water

▲ Name _____

Keeping cold

You will need: four small plastic bags; ice cubes; a collection of materials to wrap the bags in, for example, a woollen blanket, newspaper, foil, pieces of polythene; a timer.

Work with a friend.

Who can make an ice cube last the longest?

▲ Put one ice cube in each plastic bag.

▲ Put a different material round three of the bags. Do not put anything around the fourth bag.

▲ Put all the bags in the same place. Leave them for 15 minutes.

▲ Which bag kept the ice cubes the coolest?

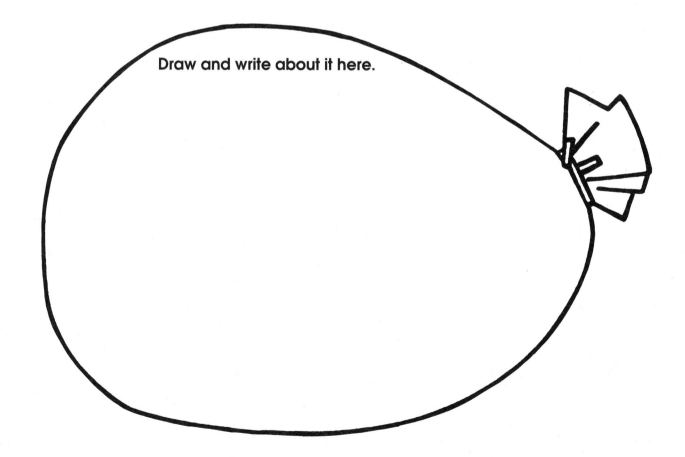

Draw and write about it here.

▲ How do you keep food cool when you go on a picnic?

▲ Name _____

An ice cube melting

You will need: ice cubes; warm water; salt; a mixture of salt and sand; small bowls; a timer.

▲ Put an ice cube on a saucer in a warm place. Look at it every few minutes. How long did it take to melt?

▲ How do you think you could melt an ice cube quickly? Try out your own ideas.

▲ Put an ice cube in each of the four bowls.

▲ Add warm water to one, salt to another, a mixture of sand and salt to another and nothing to the fourth.

▲ Put on the timer. How long does each ice cube take to melt? Which melts the quickest?

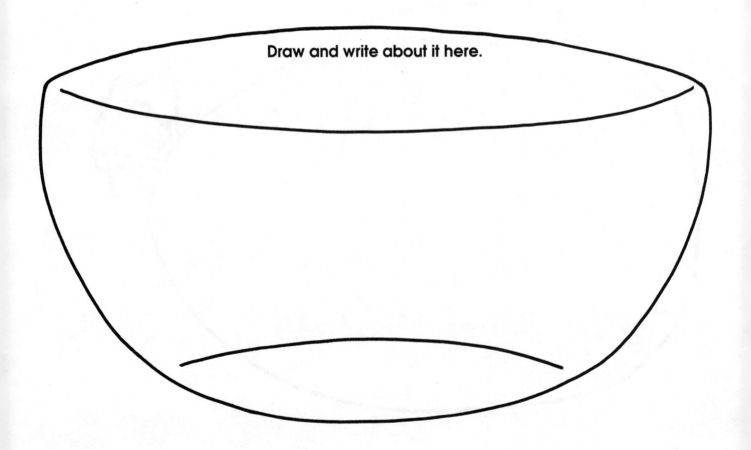

Draw and write about it here.

▲ ESSENTIALS FOR SCIENCE: Water

▲ Name _____

Dissolving things in water

You will need: clear plastic beakers; a spoonful of some of the following: salt, sugar, soil, sand, clay, custard powder, flour, bicarbonate of soda, rice, cocoa.

Work with a friend.

▲ Put a spoonful of each substance in a beaker of water.

▲ Look closely at what happens.

▲ Leave them for a day.

▲ The next day, look again and record what happened.

These things dissolved   **These things did not dissolve**

▲ ESSENTIALS FOR SCIENCE: Water

Dilute a drink

You will need: a liquid measure (you could use a large spoon or an egg-cup); concentrated orange juice; a jug of water; clear plastic beakers.

▲ Pour a measure of concentrated orange juice into a beaker. What does it look like? How does it taste?

▲ Pour a measure of juice and a measure of water into the next beaker. What changes do you notice?

▲ Pour one measure of juice and two measures of water into the next beaker. Check the taste and colour.

▲ Add measures of water until you have found the mixture you like best. How many measures of water to one measure of juice did it need?

▲ Draw and label what you did.

▲ Are there any other concentrated-drink flavours you could try?

▲ Name _____

Floating and sinking

You will need: a collection of different objects; a jug of water; paper towels.

▲ Put the objects in water one at a time.

▲ Find out which ones float and which ones sink.

▲ Draw and label the objects to make a set of things which float and a set of things which sink.

▲ What kinds of things float?

▲ What kinds of things sink?

▲ ESSENTIALS FOR SCIENCE: Water

▲ Name _____

Pushing water

You will need: a small ball; a large ball; a bucket half-filled with water; a pencil.

▲ Mark the level of water in the bucket.

▲ Float the small ball in the water.

▲ Push the ball under the water. What do you feel?

▲ What happens to the water level in the bucket?

▲ Now float the large ball in the bucket.

▲ Push the ball under the water. What do you feel?

▲ What happens to the water level in the bucket?

▲ Which ball did you have to push the hardest to make it go under the water?

▲ Which ball made the water level in the bucket change the most?

▲ ESSENTIALS FOR SCIENCE: Water

▲ Name _____

Jets of water

You will need: two plastic squeezy bottles; masking tape; scissors; a large nail; a hammer.

Ask an adult to help you.

▲ Use the nail to make a hole near the base in one bottle and near the top in the other.

▲ Seal the holes with masking tape.

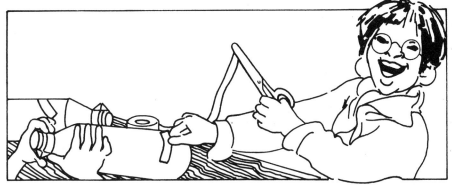

▲ Fill the bottles with water and stand them outside.

▲ Peel off the masking tape from one bottle. What happens?

▲ Peel off the masking tape from the other. Does the same thing happen?

▲ On the bottles below draw how the water came out of the two holes.

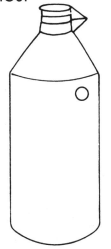 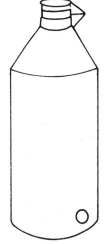

▲ Why were the jets of water different?

▲ What happens if you put a hole in the middle of the bottle?

▲ ESSENTIALS FOR SCIENCE: Water

▲ Name _____

Does water help things to grow?

You will need: seeds such as nasturtiums, peas or cress; two small jars filled with soil; plastic film.

▲ Put some seeds on the soil in both beakers.

▲ Water the soil in one of the beakers.

▲ Put plastic film over each beaker and place them in good light, but not direct sunlight.

▲ What do you think will happen?

▲ Look each day.

▲ Record what happens on the drawings below.

▲ What does this tell you about growing seeds?

▲ ESSENTIALS FOR SCIENCE: Water

Do plants take up water?

You will need: a stick of celery; a white flower such as a daisy; food colouring; a clear container; a knife.

Ask an adult to help you.

▲ Pour some water into the container.

▲ Add a few drops of food colouring.

▲ Put the stick of celery in the water.

▲ Put the container in a warm place. Leave it for about an hour.

▲ Now cut across the stem of the celery stick. What do you see?

▲ Cut across the stem in other places.

▲ Try the same thing using the white flower.

▲ What have you found out? Draw and write about it here.

▲ Name _____

What did you drink today?

We need to drink water to stay healthy. The liquids we drink contain large amounts of water.

▲ Look at the pictures below.

▲ Colour the pictures of things you like to eat or drink.

▲ Add your own ideas on the back of this sheet.

▲ Make a record of all the drink you have in one day.

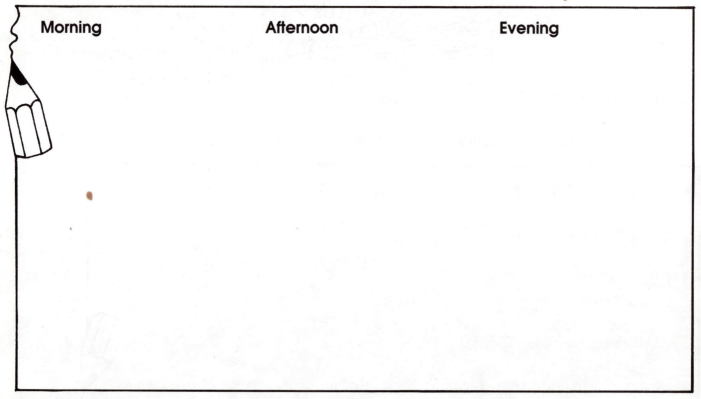

▲ Can you find out about how many litres this adds up to?

▲ ESSENTIALS FOR SCIENCE: Water

▲ Name _____

Make a water filter

You will need: a jug of water; a spoonful of garden soil; a flowerpot; some gravel or small stones; sand; a coffee filter paper or kitchen roll; a clear beaker; cotton wool.

Work with a friend.

▲ Stir the garden soil into the jug of water.

▲ Make a filter like this:

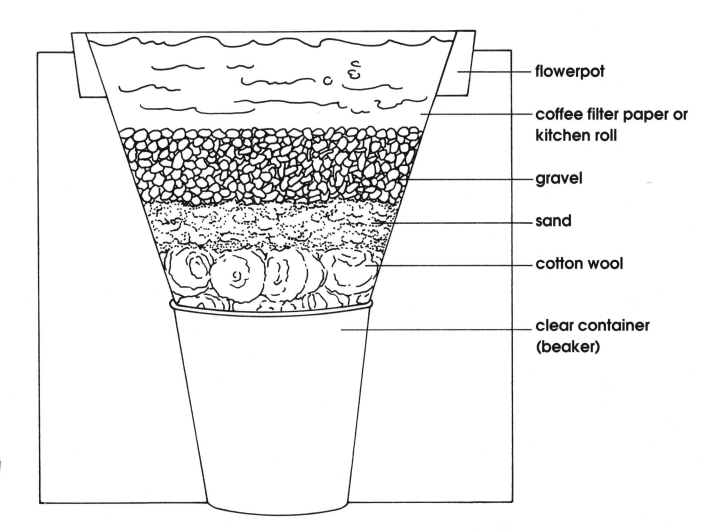

▲ Pour the muddy water slowly through the filter.

▲ What does the water look like now?

Remember that the water is not clean enough to drink or use for washing.

▲ Name _____

Water in our homes

Work with a friend.

▲ Look at the picture below.

▲ Imagine that water is blue. Colour in blue all the water in the pipes and where water is being used in the home.

▲ Colour the used water grey.

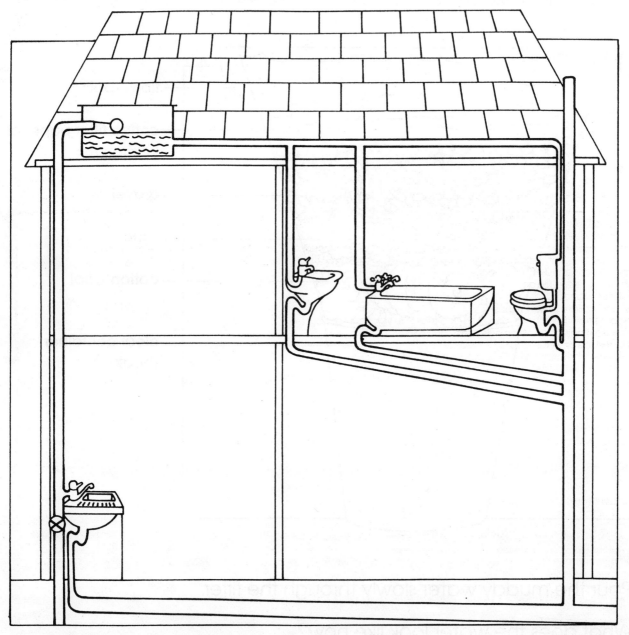

▲ Find out where the clean water comes from.

▲ Find out where used water goes to.

▲ ESSENTIALS FOR SCIENCE: Water